WASHING WINDOWS?
Irish Women Write Poetry

For the indefahgable Joan,
without whom we wouldn't be
here.
        Love,
        Carole & Lila

Eavan Boland

1980s Ireland: At Arlen House/WEB writing workshops Eavan Boland mentored and encouraged women to send out their work for feedback and publication. At one workshop a writer was reluctant to 'go public'. She said she couldn't tell her neighbours she was a poet because they would think she didn't wash her windows.

Catherine Rose
founder & publisher of Arlen House & Women's Education Bureau

An Arlen House 40th birthday anthology

WASHING WINDOWS?
Irish Women Write Poetry

in honour of
Eavan Boland
and
Catherine Rose

ARLEN
HOUSE

WASHING WINDOWS?
Irish Women Write Poetry

is published in 2017 by
ARLEN HOUSE
42 Grange Abbey Road
Baldoyle, Dublin 13, Ireland
Phone: 00 353 86 8207617
arlenhouse@gmail.com
arlenhouse.blogspot.com

Distributed internationally by
SYRACUSE UNIVERSITY PRESS
621 Skytop Road, Suite 110
Syracuse, NY 13244–5290
Phone: 315–443–5534
Fax: 315–443–5545
supress@syr.edu
syracuseuniversitypress.syr.edu

ISBN 978–1–85132–179–7, paperback

Edited and devised by Alan Hayes

cover image by Pauline Bewick
'Chinese Love Poem'
(private collection)
is reproduced courtesy of the artist

www.paulinebewick.ie

CONTENTS

51	Sinéad Gleeson
53	Anita Gracey
54	Mary Guckian
55	Christine Hammond
56	Aideen Henry
57	Phyl Herbert
58	Maura Johnston
59	Maeve Kelly
60	Wilma Kenny
61	Therese Kieran
63	Susan Knight
64	Ann Leahy
65	Anne Le Marquand Hartigan
66	Mary Madec
68	Jennifer Matthews
69	Máighréad Medbh
71	Geraldine Mills
72	Geraldine Mitchell
73	Geraldine Montague
74	Mary Montague
76	Teri Murray
78	Emma Must
79	Joan McBreen
80	Aoibheann McCann
81	Shirley McClure
82	Mamo McDonald
83	Vivienne McKechnie
84	Ellie Rose McKee
85	Maria McManus
86	Denise Nagle
87	Joan Newmann
88	Kate Newmann
90	Úna Ní Cheallaigh
91	Dairena Ní Chinneide
93	Nuala Ní Chonchúir
95	Colette Ní Ghallchóir
97	Doireann Ní Ghríofa
99	Colette Nic Aodha

PUBLISHING WOMEN

Alan Hayes

This anthology is a snapshot of the contemporary writing scene among Irish women who write poetry, and is compiled in honour of the 'foremothers' who, from the 1970s onwards, developed opportunities for women to express themselves creatively and publicly. Inspired by the original policies and publishing strands of Arlen House, this book focuses on new and emerging writers, alongside established names and reclaimed writers whose work had been lost to history. It is a unique honour to publish the first poems of many writers in this collection, alongside a poem from Edna O'Brien, the biggest name in Irish literature and one of the greatest international writers of the past century. This anthology is the beginning of a larger project to map the breadth of talent among Irish writers who are women.

Arlen House was originally founded by Catherine Rose in 1975 and that September in Galway she published her first book, *The Female Experience: The Story of the Woman Movement in Ireland*. Interestingly, Virago, the world's most famous feminist press, also published their first book in London in September 1975, Mary Chamberlain's *Fenwomen: A Portrait of Women in an English Village*; however, *The Female Experience* was the more radically feminist of the two books. Arlen House's second book in 1977 was Janet Martin's *The Essential Guide for Women in Ireland*, which left both writer and publisher liable to a fine and imprisonment for providing information on contraception and abortion.

Catherine Rose moved to Dublin in 1978 and quickly expanded the press with three new worker-directors joining: Janet Martin, former women's page editor of the *Irish Independent*, Terry Prone, communications expert, and Dr Margaret Mac Curtain (Sr Benvenuta), historian and educator, who published her *Women in Irish Society: The Historical Dimension* (1978) with Arlen House, the first Irish women's history book, which became a massive success. Later, other people connected to the press included Mary Cullen, Ann Murphy, Eleanor Murphy, Janet Madden-Simpson and Louise Barry (Louise C. Callaghan).

In 1978, prominent poet and critic Eavan Boland also became involved as an associate editor, working on the first ever creative writing competition for women in Ireland, which was judged by Eavan, Mary Lavin and David Marcus. The resulting book, *The Wall Reader*, became a No. 1 bestseller in 1979. It contained a spirited introduction by Eavan on the concept of the 'woman writer' and marginalisation, and the need to mainstream great writing into the Irish canon. The book received a backlash from sections of the media, yet was a huge success and spanned two more annual competitions and anthologies. The second, published as *A Dream Recurring* (1980), was also judged by Eavan and included poetry as well as short stories, with a third anthology, *The Adultery*, appearing in 1982.

By the 1970s Eavan was already regarded internationally as one of the most outstanding young Irish poets, with her second collection, *The War Horse*, being published in London in 1975 by Gollancz (in autumn 1980 Arlen House reissued *The War Horse* in paperback and hardback). Arlen House in early 1980 published *In Her Own Image* with drawings by Constance Short. Quite simply, this book, along with 1982's *Night Feed*, changed the face of Irish literature. Although met with some media silence and ignorance, these books were major successes and opened up new pathways in Irish poetry.

In 1980, Eavan became editor of the newly-created Popular Classics series, and wrote the introduction to Kate O'Brien's novel, *The Ante-Room*, which led to a revival of that neglected writer's work. She spoke at the first Kate O'Brien Weekend in Limerick in 1984 which Arlen House organised to mark the tenth anniversary of Kate O'Brien's death.

In 1984, Arlen House founded Women's Education Bureau (WEB), the national organisation for women writers, with Eavan Boland as creative director. WEB organised the Annual Workshop for Women Writers, workshops around the country and the Writers and Readers Day, alongside research, advice and mentoring services. It had a large membership, published a newsletter and launched, in 1987, the first issue of a journal, *The WEB: New Writing by Women*. Eavan Boland was the general editor, with guest editors Mary Rose Callaghan and Evelyn Conlon. Reflecting on earlier WEB workshops since 1984, Eavan wrote: "it struck me too often and too forcibly that women had to struggle at a physical and metaphysical level to be writers in this country". A WEB writing group still exists in Dublin to the present day.

In December 1986, Arlen House launched *The Journey and Other Poems*, a co-publication with Carcanet who published in the UK in February 1987. And in autumn 1989 Carcanet published, "in association with WEB", Eavan's *Selected Poems*, with WEB organising a media and advertising campaign in Ireland to promote the book. Catherine Rose had worked as co-ordinator of the National Year on Ageing and in 1990 she founded and became CEO of Age and Opportunity, the national body promoting creativity in older people. Thus Arlen House and WEB came to a natural end – that is until, in 2000, Arlen House was relaunched by myself, with encouragement from Catherine Rose and Margaret Mac Curtain – but that's another story entirely.

Eavan Boland's career and reputation has continued to grow internationally and she has added substantially to her body of work. It is an honour for Arlen House to publish in 2016 a major collection of essays and poems, *Eavan Boland: Inside History,* edited by Siobhan Campbell and Nessa O'Mahony. Catherine Rose retired recently from Age and Opportunity and lives in Dublin. She is Ireland's first feminist publisher and has made a monumental contribution to the lives of women and in creating change in Irish society.

Washing Windows? Irish Women Write Poetry, compiled in honour of Eavan Boland and Catherine Rose, is a wide-ranging, inspiring, moving and insightful collection of poetry by contemporary Irish writers who are women and who have something to say.

Arlen House
Dublin/Galway/Syracuse, NY

WASHING WINDOWS?
Irish Women Write Poetry

Pauline Bewick

SCAN

The CT brain scan's normal,
the lumber spine is worn,
the cholesterol level is far too high,
when three to five's the norm.
The blood count's very normal,
the kidney's normal too,
the liver seems to function well,
and the sugar levels too.
We'll wait for the fine tune MRI,
it's then we'll know the score
and a few more tests will see you through
so off on a trolley you'll go.
Down corridors blue with a dangling shoe
and into a very long spaceship,
do not panic I say to myself,
lie flat and still on this spaceship shelf.
Engine on – off like a bomb,
the rattling noise is shockingly strong.
An awful fear that things will go wrong
so I thought of this MRI wrapping song.
Go, go, go, go, go,
whatever, whatever, whatever,
you're wrong, you're wrong, you're wrong, you're wrong,
no never, no never, no never,
you're strong, you're strong, you're strong, you're strong,
whatever, whatever, whatever,
no, no, no, no,
no never, no never, no never,
go, go, go, go,
be clever, be clever, be clever.
You're on your own
on a spaceship throne
forever, forever, forever.

Maureen Boyle

LATIN LESSON

I am studying Latin again, the language lost in Loreto
when we learned the meaning of irony and had to choose
between it and the study of history. Our teacher
was first a young man we all thought handsome
our first words out of Ecce Romani, *puella, puellae*
the conjugation *amo amas amat* said with feeling.

Now I see him pimply and pale but our young hearts ran
      off with him
when he ran off, leaving his wife, our geography teacher, bereft.
Then it was an older bent-backed crone who passed our desks
in a dusty black robe, strange and wizened, otherworldly
like a character in the villa we were reading about. But
she was gentle and took us into the lives of Falvia and Cordelia.

And now out the window I am watching a wagtail
dance in the neighbour's slick new gutter.
He is a flash of yellow and he is dancing in the drain.
I think first he is the passerine *moticalla flava*
the *yellow moving tail* but then, no, he is
the more modest *moticalla cinerea*

and even with his yellow streak suncaught
amongst the bright October leaves of a hornbeam
and a birch his name, there in the gutter
he has maybe taken for a rushing stream,
is derived from dust or ashes, *cinera,*
from which we get the word *incinerate.*

Clodagh Brennan Harvey

SHEDDING

Don't you ever wonder
        if we are merely fooled
        when we think
        snakes shed
        their skins
        painlessly?

What if
        that elegant,
        silky web
        they leave behind –
        revealed by
        a translucent shimmer
        among plangent
        scattered leaves –
        really only
        belies an agony
        of rebirth?

Is it not so with us
        when a cold
        winter's realisation
        sets in;
        when the only way through
        to the far-off warmth
        of spring
        means shedding
        our barren skin;
        not extinction,
        not self-immolation,
        just a frantic,
        instinctual clawing out
        towards new air?

Deirdre Brennan

EXPOSÉ

The story out on him,
the extent of his abuse of children
over the long years spread from mouth to mouth,
they drew a cloak around him to shield him.
And now the child, in the polished convent parlour
betrayed by the nuns' accepting
the priest's visits to her,
when they knew what was going on.
But no sound was heard from the closed room,
the pathetic screams of the girl stifled by him
when he, like a fierce sparrow hawk
pierced the pigeon in his talons.

They moved him from country to country,
diocese to diocese,
city to city,
where he prowled school corridors,
and hospital wards
in search of his prey,
warrant after warrant on him
deferred, waiting for an answer.

There is little heard these days
from the monastery on the hill
but the keening wind
under the eaves,
the abbot who sheltered the errant priest
befuddled by the problem
retired from his position,
a new abbot installed
begging our forgiveness.

NOCHTADH

An scéal amuigh air,
méid na mí-úsáide a bhain sé as páistí
thar na blianta sceite ó bhéal go béal
dhruideadar ina bhfalang timpeall
chun fóirithinte air.
Is anois an páiste i bparlús snasta an chlochair
ar ar imir na mná rialta feall
ag glacadh le cuairteanna an tsagairt uirthi
nuair ab fheasach dóibh cad a bhí ar siúl.
Is gíog ná míog ní raibh ón seomra iata sin,
scread léanmhar an chailín maolaithe aige
nuair a thráigh sé í, spioróg fhíochmhar
le colúr ina chrúcaí.

D'aistríodar ó thír go tír é,
ó fhairche go fairche,
ó chathair go cathair,
eisean ag smúrthacht thart
ar dhorchlaí scoile
is bardanna ospidéil ar thóir a chreiche
barántas i ndiaidh barántais air
scaoilte thart ag feitheamh ar fhreagra.

Níl smid le cloisint na laethe seo
ón mainistir ar an gcnoc
ach éagaoin na gaoithe
faoi na sceimhleacha;
an t-ab a thug dídean don sagart in earráid,
mearaithe leis an gceist,
éirithe as a phost,
ab nua i réim ag impí maithiúnais orainn.

Mary Rose Callaghan

COMPASS
for Bob

I still see you on buses, or sitting in pubs.
Walking home late you often meet me,
scolding the way you did when I refused taxis.
I only know you're gone when entering the house
I switch on the light and go to bed with BBC4.

But clearing out your ancient Morris Minor,
(in the garage, smelling of oil and old leather;
the car you joked you'd save before me in a fire,
and now nudge me to sell, or do something with),
your compass is there among old AA maps.

Remember the day we walked the Wicklow Way?
I had studied the guidebook, which said turn left
at the stile by the crooked tree and the funny stones.
But you held up the compass. 'You're going *back*!'
I argued, sure I was right, but no, you were.

I'm trying to write this poem for years
but grief choked me the way ivy was killing
trees in the garden you loved. On Saturday
I yanked it all off, brought bags to the dump,
but kept your compass to show the way.

Siobhan Campbell

WEEDING

When you weed a field, bend over the long root suckers,
the weeders moving in a line across the ridges,
a stippled human stripe of inclined heads against
the ordered rippling rows of mangels,
then the world seems right and we are in our place.

When you refuse to weed and hang out with a friend
under the dreeping willow in the bend that is not ploughed
where no grass grows over the stones and what is buried,
you watch the workers easing themselves to night;
its shadow keeps ahead of them as they cross.

Then you might think of sacrifice or the greater good
but you don't, flirty with heat as heat leaves the day
and you separate, seeing things anew, filthy
with possibility. It's too late now to join the weeding crew.
And the willow laughs its long thin laugh at you.

Moya Cannon

OCTOBER 1945

It was two months later
two months after a small sun
opened its belly over the city
and pressed Hiroshima into the ground.

After two months of trudging
and turning rubble she found it
under a melted bottle – her daughter's
scorched wooden sandal.
There was no mistaking the straps
she had made from her old kimono.

Ruth Carr

BIRCH AND HAW TREE
Dorothy Wordsworth and Mary Ann McCracken

They started out secure in similar soil.

One, uprooted early, leaned to home
towards a certain light, grew sensitive
to rain, to every bird that sang among
her leaves, to insect wings and northern
winds and every fragile nesting.
A tree that bloomed her silvery best

within another's shadow.

The other stayed quite small
but tough, rebuffed prevailing winds
and when her closest was cut down
wove her branches tight as hedge
a hiding place, a shelter.
Feared as the haw left standing in the field,
she stood her thorny ground.

Aoife Casby

I WANT

I want to have fun.
I want to sell my yellow dress.
I want to exchange my Braun mixer for a secondhand iPhone.
I want to begin talking,
say, about hermaphroditism,
then, by way of fraught elections
and misunderstood referenda,
end up on nude philosophers.
I want to collect all the things
from the ditches of long ago
I never did
and really look at them:
tin cans, torn clothes, silk
stockings, weeds, pages
from an unidentified book,
the plastic skeletal remains
of a 2-tailed kite,
the fright on your face
when you heard about
Three Mile Island,
how years like that
change the history of accident,
how we have no history
but ourselves.
I want to sell my yellow dress
even though
it is the only clothing that I own.
I want to have fun.
I will pack a bag
and put into it all that is mine:
nothing.
I am weightless.

I overhear conversations, take hugs,
still have room for more.
Did you think about my face
when you heard
there was a shooting
next door?

Eileen Casey

WHITE FENCES MAKE GOOD NEIGHBOURS

I'm painting the fences white, shed too,
white as a gumdrop or a wedding shoe.

When that's done I'll float in a summer palace
canopied by pale-leaved whitebeam trees,
lie on a blanket with my ice-coloured cat,
eat cake, be cooled by spigots of light.

I'll read about Antarctica while butterflies
ripen like berries, ignore warning telegrams
pipped by a blackbird
three tiers up at least.

I'll be whitening out lawnmowers, chainsaws,
barking feuds, a neighbourhood's graffiti of sound.

Sarah Clancy

In the Distance

from chin on hair mornings
we are diluted across
each blue, blue day
with our useless histories
as faint-hearted and wispy
as an afternoon moon

across the bay then
in the evening glowlight
childhoods wane
and on just this type
of seeplight summer night
pale adolescence tangles
in our breath and we
are neither here nor there

but later in the wanderdark
and the redfade
of our warm bed
with its leg on leg on hip
we let no other versions in
we sleep oblivious
to the heron at the shoreline
to the one
illuminated car passing,

in ignorance of the fat moth
tricked by lamplight
and dying in the kitchen
we persist,
on nights like this
we stretch out before ourselves
we stretch into the distance ...

Jane Clarke

COPPER SOLES
i.m. Shirley McClure

In an old Finnish story
the hero must build a boat from oak

to bear him home through a raging storm
but he cannot complete his work

without three magic words;
the first will secure the stern,

the second will fasten the ledges,
the third will ready the forecastle.

To find the words
he must walk across points of needles,

edges of hatchets,
blades of swords,

for which he needs shoes
with copper soles.

Dear friend,
while the doctors chase pain

around your body,
where will we find such a cobbler?

Mary Coll

SILVER

How far can I go with this before I scare you?
I'd better not say that you are all my joy, all of it,
you'd find that too ridiculous, and laugh,
or that I still watch you sleeping, sometimes,
because that's just too weird.
I won't mention how hard I fight the urge
to hold you back
almost every time you go to leave,
for school, or the cinema, or walk the dog,
only almost, though,
I mean I'm not that crazy, really.
I know you'll come back later,
later than we agreed, always,
but then what if you don't,
where would I take myself then?
Maybe that empty car park on the outskirts
of madness where nobody hears me banging
my head on the horn, over and over,
because my throat is too raw from howling,
and there are no tears left,
not even the dust of a tear in the duct of my eye,
refusing to silence my grief.
Who would do that, you ask, horrified,
strolling away from the table,
trailing crumbs in your wake.
Me, I don't say, to your immense relief,
reminding you instead to put the lid on the jam
and call me, please, because you are the star attraction
in the circus I never ran away to,
spinning effortlessly without a net,
while I watch, with one eye closed in terror, the other wide
open in amazement, seeing you sparkle like silver,
terrified you'll catch your death of cold in that costume.

Natasha Cuddington

from PRINT

hang the stiff apron on the body Near the hand.

And Battered cotton of a thousandsleepssheets /

      Preserved in stack-forms

        to ripshred& douse

with Spirits. Wipe Hands,

 keep Surface

free from form.

                      On print day,

                When Boys are to school&

Men at work,

I come to Labour Mine /   That is not Theirs,

Glad-rags exchanged for utility,

Tied with cord.

Bríd Cummins

LOVE'S CLOAK

I didn't know what came to me
in love's cloak.
It sat on the stairs and waited;
so anxious to meet me,
so keen to truss me up,
to influence every moment.
It waited around corners
crouched in doorways, ready
to spring on my unsuspecting
vulnerability.
It crawled through the long grass
on sticky summer nights, and
sat by the river on frozen winter
afternoons, when fools venture out.
It held me close.

On dusty city streets
there it was again, with
a mysterious look from dark eyes
under a dipped hat.
It followed me through parks
and flattered me with offers
of the high life.
For short periods I succumbed,
but never comfortable
with disguise.

Paula Cunningham

CROSSROADS

This is the place where nothing ever happens,
where youngsters cram into their souped-up cars
to swig and laugh and drive each other crazy,
they maybe can't afford the drink in bars.

This is the place where doughnuts spin on handbrakes,
where young men howl and hit each other hard,
this is the place that's Hades on a weekend,
where daylight's quiet, loudness seeks the dark.

Where daylight's quiet loudness finds the dark –
the place become a Hades every weekend –
where young ones roar and punch each other hard.
This is the place they revved and honed their doughnuts,

perhaps they felt unwelcome in the bars
(the horseplay'd only drive their elders crazy)
and chose instead the harbour of their cars.
This is the place where nothing's meant to happen,
the junction spinning under April stars.

Celia de Fréine

AT LAST
*Go where never before**

When he thought of going to that place
he'd never been in before
he understood it would be there he'd be based
no matter where that was
giving to understand he was expecting
to arrive somewhere – somewhere new –

most important of all: he understood.

As for those who knew him
who'd spent years working with him
who realised he was an ordinary man –
more than that – that he had a sense of humour –
when they didn't come to visit him

there was no one to debate this with

apart from the two nurses
who were used to the like –
their words of solace echoing to the heavens
as they dispensed compassion
when all that was left to him was this thought
spinning in his head

just as he was about to reach his destination.

from a poem written by Samuel Beckett before he died

AR DEIREADH
*Go where never before**

Agus é ag smaoineamh ar dhul chuig an áit úd
nach raibh sé inti cheana
tuigeadh dó gurbh ansin a mbeadh sé lonnaithe
ba chuma cén áit í
ag tabhairt le fios go raibh súil aige
áit éicint a bhaint amach – áit úrnua –

an rud ba thábhachtaí: tuigeadh dó

Maidir leo siúd a raibh aithne acu air
a chaith na blianta ag obair in éindí leis
a d'aithin gur ghnáthfhear é –
níos mó ná sin – go raibh cumas grinn ann –
nuair nár tháinig siad ar cuairt chuige

ní raibh éinne lena bhféadfaí é seo a phlé

seachas an bheirt altra
a raibh taithí acu ar a leithéid –
a bhfocla sólásacha ag baint macalla as na spéartha
trua agus taise á mbronnadh acu air
nuair nach raibh fágtha ach an smaoineamh seo
ag castáil ina chloigeann

é díreach ar tí a cheann scríbe a bhaint amach

* ó dhán a scríobh Samuel Beckett sular cailleadh é

Annie Deppe

AND WHEN THE RED WINE FROM MINERVOIS

And when the red wine from Minervois
turned out to be white,
my guard let down, the word slipped out,
'I need to bring the *worsh* in from the line'.
How many years has it been?
I must have been all of seven when I realized
only my mother, brought up in Bryn Mawr,
ever spoke of *worsh* cloths.

Soon I could say wash with the best of them.
Wash the dishes, do the wash,
my father reminding me always
to wash between my legs.
The washcloth strategically floating
over him during our shared baths.

There are so many things I never
managed to tell you, Mother,
and my shame over your accent
was undeniably the least.

I will bring in the *worsh* from the line tonight,
I will make up my marriage bed,
I will rejoice in the sun calves
frolicking the cliff road above the sea,
I will try and find the right words to say
what has never been said.

Moyra Donaldson

ICELAND

I went to her with stories and poems
of horses and rain and how I've stood
on the wild edges of my own island
where the land falls off into the Atlantic;
how I've lived with flocks of black birds,
borrowed feathers, dreams, bone voices.

I found in her a sister dreaming space,
an icy voice, a looking glass to step through,
rain to snow, crow to raven, trot to tölt,
river to ice and everywhere her forty
shades of white; light so keen it fills
my eye with blood and every snow storm
with its own song; choirs of glacier and rock,
bone murmurings on Thingvellir plain,
the language strange, but the sound
familiar, lifted and fluted on the wind.

Then I stood in the rift between continents,
clear and immense; inexorable breath
of a power that knows only its own story.

                *

Necrosis shows like a snow cloud
on cat scan images of his brain; stroke.
Blood fissure deep in the substance splits
the future from itself; my legs trembling
as they trembled in her cold exhalation.

Katie Donovan

Stories

The giant dappled squid
lives deep and dark,
away from the eyes of men.
But stories proclaim
of a sailor, caught
by a huge tentacle
that swung across his boat
and clasped him, tight.

So the tensile grip of my desire
swims in her silent haunt.
Do not be surprised
if, one day, her terrible need
forces her into the light,
and with one long swipe,
she takes you, whole.

Mary Dorcey

MAKING

Not therapy – this poetry making –
it is something more like
shaping or carving
something physical,
making a poem
you could better say,
resembles
moulding
something,
actual,
what it may be like
to make
for instance –
a small
three-legged stool –
a sturdy,
smooth-skinned
inconspicuous,
reliable
seat
of polished
wood.
To set it
on uneven ground
between busy, useful
lives –
to say – you might find
a service
for this –
you could sit
down on it
for a moment or two –

You might rest
for a while.
It might bear your weight.

Micheline Egan

THREE GOOD HAIL MARYS

When I picked the priest
with the late vocation
to confess my sin of adultery,
I knew exactly
what I was doing.

I wanted a man of the cloth
who had tasted
the flesh of a woman
and knew that love
was all it promised to be
– a taste of the divine.

Clemency Emmet

THE WIDOW

I started life bare as a sapling.
Gradually my branches spread,
some crooked, some straight.
My roots grew far down,
I bore fruit.

For many a long year
I stood against wind and storm,
glorying in the weight of my leaves.
Children and children's children,
till loss cleft me.

I now am chilled as if by frost.
My trailing branches will not root.
Let me stay bare as I began.
There is less pain that way
for when I fall.

Martina Evans

LIFE CALLS FOR DEATH

I take my broom
to the lost wisteria blossoms
that rained down in yesterday's
fast wind like snow.

Donny crunches a ladybird
when we sit in the sun.
I shudder thinking about it
as I open his can of John West.

The wren calls and a blackbird
sings, the cats stare up
making kkk kkk noises.

Later Donny is at the end
of the path,
feathers flutter down from
his mouth like black snow.

Carole Farnan

FALLEN WOMAN

A dancehall fall
ran you aground
at my father's startled feet
amid a sea of G.I.s
and started the whole thing.

A staircase fall
made me slip my moorings
and move early into life,
impatient to be born.

Following your footloose ways
I surfaced often to your anxious face
after many a street fall
over a flagstone or feather.

I stumbled, tottered and tumbled
through untethered teens,
cascaded down staircases
in impossible heels till

middle-age grounded me in flats
(now no hope of walking tall)
but still l fall:
a hostage to my genes,
lacking your ballast.

Tanya Farrelly

IGNITION

On cold winter mornings
when the car wouldn't start,
my mother got under the hood
to cajole whatever lived there.

Pulling the ragged blanket
off the sleeping engine,
she dried spark plugs, tried leads,
encouraged it with words.

Shivering in the driver's seat,
my five-year-old fingers turned
the key, and we both listened
as the engine moaned, coughed
and caught.

Erin Fornoff

THE WAY I SLEEP NOW

It could be the skew of jet lag,
where a body can't catch up
to the technology that moves it.
I've flown back to find
it's already autumn here,
the corners of night pulled tighter in.
Or it could be the body asserting itself
in a foreign routine become
familiar, absent the fear of going.
Before I left I'd spend half the night
pressing my face at different angles
into the pillow to find the one
that would tip me into darkness.
I'd list whatever lapse and shortcoming
may have bloomed this punishment.
Since I've returned though my mind is
bright with awareness later than usual.
I'm sleeping like I have a masters degree in sleep,
the kind you have to rub off and creep from,
like I've met a man in an office
and made an arrangement for rest
that requires a journey in and out.

Orfhlaith Foyle

TELL ME YOU ARE ALL STILL ALIVE

Made the Belfast train with two minutes to spare.
Bus lazy and late!
Sitting in Dundalk now, doors open and wind
blowing. Hope you are all resting.
A man diseased by Parkinson's
stabs his fingers
into a tin-foil sandwich.
Don't look at his wife. She has turned into his mother.
He dribbles coffee onto his jumper.
This is love gone to rust.
Hope you are all resting. A whistle goes but the train stays still.
The man with Parkinson's had his childhood on a farm
in Nottingham with some cows and bright, delightful pigs.
Speak up. Speak up. She can't hear you. It was the
chemicals there, dear, on the farm, with the cows
and the bright, delightful pigs.
He lifts his hand. His face wobbles in the dark light.
All that time and he was being destroyed, wasn't he?
His mother is one hundred and three.
The Queen sent a card.
We live long, the man says.
There are people on the platform. They look in with different-
sized faces.
Very long, the man says.
He lifts his coffee cup. It spills through his fingers.
His wife's lipstick is dark and cold.
But we die, don't we, dear?
The Dundalk skies knuckle onto the train while I text:
The wind is dark and old. My phone is losing battery.
Tell me you are all still alive.

Susie Fry

ISLANDS

Below, there is an emerald
patch stitched with stones
on land ribbed with memory.

Two ravens call and tumble
and from behind the cairn a hare appears
then disappears to lead us on

to the white-washed church, where the caretaker's dog
watches a woman pray, while those that came
the usual way pose for photos in the mist.

There are moments of mauve and turquoise,
pale sands and the islands revealed, then taken
with the sweeping cloud.

Out west, no line divides sea from sky.
They rise again from polished steel:
Inishturk, Achillbeg, Bofin, Clare.

Peggie Gallagher

REEK SUNDAY

1

Broken stone under my feet, mist,
and the descent of pilgrims
who'd set out at midnight.
I remember father joining the pilgrims,
the soda-bread sandwiches mother handed him.

We were small, we had lessons,
we heard the pen and ink skritch
of mother's airmail letters.

We had yet to hear sounds
of departure, a bus station,
how a kitchen chair creaks, relentless,
where grief rocks itself.

2

The boulder crest is a breath of cold light.
Pilgrims filling the scoop, knees pressed
on stone, the pale ankle bone burned
with an imprint of roads they have travelled.

Still they come, grouped round the periphery
in huddled clumps of overcoats and rosaries,
children among them.
It was here the saint lured the serpents,
then caused them to plunge to their death
down the sheer southern ridge.

The Mass bell's high-flung notes
pour down – a salve,
a rippled chalice.

This wind-honed high altar,
its ancient trodden path
tapers like memory.
As the year tilts past the hinge,
days slip from the page,
the mouth of the bay far below,
its packed school of drumlins
swimming out from the shore.

Dani Gill

BALLOON

I used to think of you
panicked, like a child who had
let the string slip

and up and up you went
before I could know, that
I had let you go.

Sinéad Gleeson

At Kinlough Lighthouse

Last night, lightning knocked out the beam
and we hoped, like city folk, it would happen again.
In darkness, foam lashed on glassy rock,
waves heaved, and something called to you.

A mile off land,
selkies are raising sandbanks
making graves for young bones.

Lighthouses here wear black
and yellow bands, daymarks of
mourning and sickness in
bumblebee shades.
But spring feels far away,
its buds a distant cruelty.

The glass and stone sentinel
watches his fitful sleep.
Each sweep of beam over
white-washed walls
a carousel anointment, with
blessings for only some.

In sun-shingled light
we walk to a tenth-century church
its holy well peripheral, weed-choked.

On the hill, the ruin of a house, hearth cold
lintel long gone, window gaps like missing teeth.

The bay below cradles old shipwrecks, the splinter
of timber, the crack of a hull. Man overboard,

surfacing once more, salted, fighting for air.
The future is never a single beam, nor a straight,
unwavering line. You are your own lighthouse.
Out on the dark waves, you send up a flare.

Anita Gracey

HELPLESS

Amid the jarring cacophony
of Aleppo,
numbed by survival you perch
absorbed in devastation.

I want to bless you in kisses
to enfold you
to never leave you
to feed you a banquet fit for Eid
to bathe you in bubbles
to dress you in sunlit clothes
to sing you a lullaby
in your mother tongue
to cradle you on a bed of petals
pleated with angels' breath.

Instead
I tuck your image deep inside
and turn my face away
helpless.
I let the news reports drone on.

Mary Guckian

BOG COTTON

Little white flags of cotton
light up the cutaway bog.
The shivering white flames
brighten the darkness
of the centuries-old turf bank
about to be cut and dried.

Dug out with a metal slean,
the heavy sods caught and
placed on a wooden barrow,
they are turned into heaps
and spread out to dry
flattening tiny delicate buds,

later footed into twelve sods.
When the wetness is gone
they are clamped and taken
on creels to the horse and cart,
leaving bog cotton free
to rise and glow again.

Christine Hammond

THE DARK PINES

Detailed not to march
the dark pines stand
still for all time
drilled, upright
sentinel
feet on the floor
a dark pines corps.

The dark pines stand
row upon row
drilled, upright
sentinel
a mendacious corps
guarding a Tantalus
beyond a resinous door.

Through the dark pines
across the purple dunes
the indigo dusk
leaks a cruel blotter
to steal the shore
its inky plotter
willing phantoms' fingers
to draw the phizog of death.

The dark pines stand
naked in a chicane
their needles as fig leaves.
I picked and plucked
their guileless fruit
and buried it at sea
for Fibonacci to find
and set the truth free.

Aideen Henry

BESTIAL

Make him simian,
arms outstrip legs,
knuckles trail,
back-sloping brow,
small hindbrain,
hair tufts on each phalanx
of fingers and toes,
prominent lower jaw,
perioral puff out,
thin lines for lips.

He'll still give eye contact,
be sensuous, curious
finger twirling,
body hugging,
playful, attentive,
warmfleshed and enfolding,
he'll sift through your hair
for creatures and find none,
the same frenetic jog
to the summit.

No intellectual blubber,
no casting about
for meaning,
no past and
no future,
no loss
of home ground,
no entitlement,
no terms or conditions,
no fiscal creep.

Phyl Herbert

ARCHAEOLOGY OF THE SOUL

At the funeral of my youth
only one offered a cushioned
grave for my remains.

'Will you marry me?' he asked.
I was thirty then, and on the shelf.
'No', I replied and then I died.

Decades come and go. I lost two
on bread and butter glue.

Now, I'm the Big Oh ...
and have opened up myself on the shelf.
I want to dance to the tune of sex
have babies and catch up with myself.

Maura Johnston

TREE MUSIC

The flash of ash in
this bone-bare winter hedge is
in pitch-perfect key.

Here birch bark tatters
flutter, fan dancers to
a rag-time rhythm.

Right in the centre
the fairy thorn jigs in time
to a wayward wind.

And the willow droops
wind-whipped, cross-limbed, swaying in
a soft shoe shuffle.

Maeve Kelly

REFUGE

He touched me here – she said
laughing, the red hair swinging
to hide her pale surprise
and she laced her fingers
over the mound of her child
on each side again, the sphere
of her inner world concealed
and then revealed by her light
mannerly exposition.

In the centre aisle of the church
in front of all – she said – he placed
his hands here. I was mortified.
And that smile again, confused
yet awed by tribute, seemed to light
our table where we hung, silent
over empty tea cups. A child cried
in a room upstairs and one moved
to listen. Outside the orange glare
a security light zoned our limits,
a rubbish tip where horses roamed
wild as their owners, illicit nibblers
at our crooked pastures.
We here are tenants. There in the church
the priest proclaimed, not her
but her inhabitant, mysterious life.

She was bemused by this.
This spotlight on her portion,
her definable other
the source of her significance.
She hung her head, and we hung with her
speechless.

Wilma Kenny

NOTES ON THE BREAK UP

1

She was free as a little bird
pecking on a rose hip,
walking a hard path
back then.

2

We waited for the wildness
to be raked out of her.
For roots to be put down.

3

We are on a cliff edge.
Rags hang from the sky.
Damaged roof.

4

Everyone has gone away,
only birds can live here.
Will you survive the flood?
There are no curtains to keep out the dark.
No windows to keep out the rain.
Your house is broken.

Therese Kieran

GRANDPARENTS

I'm minus 7, my Granny's dead;
I am an un-fertilised egg.
My Granny is yellow and thin,
only her shell remains
where my mother stands sobbing.
I'll know her by my mother,
I'll love her by the stories handed down;
the chocolate bars and cakes
she sent to boarding school,
to daughters worth educating.

I'm 12, my Granda's dead;
I am ushered towards his coffin
in the good front room.
He's smiling, I can't think why
and surrounded by strangers I'm crying.
Crying for the circus to end.
Bewildered by a body that lies so still
while biscuits and tea float by
and a hum runs
the line of chairs along the walls.

I'm 21, my Granda's dead;
I am serving teas,
tutored by cousins twice removed.
His chin is pointed high but I'm sure
of the glint behind his shut-tight eyes.
I cry a little, laugh more;
sharing a repertoire of 96 years:
scholar, farmer, father, widower,
pipe-smoking, stick-waving poetry lover
who professed he could drink learning.

I'm 29, my Nana's dead;
my son sits on my hip,
'Nana's asleep in her cot', he says,
points to her pink angora cardigan
over a dress she wore to my wedding.
We step outside, wait with the crowd,
leave my father
to have the last look,
the last smile, the last flash of pink,
on the tips of her beaded hands.

Susan Knight

ROISIN

Roisin dreamt a poem
a poem in Irish
I must remember it
she told herself in the dream,
and she did.

What's it about? asks Josh.
Nothing, she says,
walking up a cliff
that's all
that's all.

I like to think of her poem
having her stand on a Mayo strand
looking out across the inky sea
examining strange stones
and shells and beached jellyfish.
That hank of weed spread over the sand
like a girl's wet hair.

I like to think of her
amid the grasses on the dunes.
That seed head about to pop.
Those seeds blown on the wind.
Then scrambling up the cliff side
higher and higher
her gammy leg suddenly mended.

Ann Leahy

THE ODD WORD

Because it brings to mind a thousand tedious hours
of drab constraint, as adults we demur.
Yet we'll choose an odd word to shape a phrase
(as a skew is used to taper a surface on a lathe).

'Ah, that's a thing on which he hasn't any *meas*',
we'll say (of hare-bells patterning a patch of grass;
or of a shelter-belt of thorn), meaning he is one
who fails to value what he's always known.

Because we can still yearn when long-past belief
(even if we never had faith), a ghost-word may weave
its way inside small-talk: 'I have an aul' *grá* for him',
I may say, meaning that I harbour a regard, undimmed,

something on which I should keep more *smacht*,
meaning that I'd do well to stick to facts –
turning the deaf ear, stifling the occasional start
at any sound of skittering from a bricked-up heart.

NOTE FROM IRISH:
Meas: esteem, respect, regard, value
Grá: love, affection
Smacht: discipline, control, grip
Faoi smacht: under control

Anne Le Marquand Hartigan

THE GOOD WINE
Menopause

I have poured my blood out.
Giving always.
Used it.

Curled in my womb.
Carried it. Carefully.
Forced the child out.
Bawling.

Six times this womb has filled.
It is enough.

Now I choose myself,
wisdom is my own.
Even the moon cannot tempt me,
I am full-grown.

Riches I shared so liberally
I pull these tides home.
The wine that spilled abundance
now is mine alone.

I have bred the world on,
pushed over a turning,
I am stronger than the moon,
and those thoughts that give you fear
are truer than the sun's eye.

Mary Madec

SHE LIVES EVERYDAY AS IF IT WERE HER FIRST

She has just discovered the beauty of *Sole Mio*
trips with delight on every emotional contour.

She's all *iTunes* and *Youtube* this evening, asks me to dance
to Handel's *Did You Not Hear My Lady?*

We waltz out the four-four with little steps
down the corridor of the nursing home, laughing like old times.

She looks at me lovingly and says
You are a beautiful person.

Where did we first meet?
You remind me of someone I know. I see she's intrigued.

Aah, you deserve only the best darling she says
pirouetting and proffering her wedding ring

engraved 1969. She talks of the place
where Dad gave it to her, the old music stand

in Dún Laoghaire Harbour. I hear seagulls and ship horns
in her quaking voice.

She's still with Handel and tries to sing
Beyond My Open Window, stumbles on *restless wings*.

By bedtime there is no song left in her. She's breathless,
frets over buttons which won't close;

she knows that it's a hairbrush in her hand
but she cannot brush her hair.

Suddenly on the edge, she's lucid and terrified,
there's nothing to gather up, remember after the day.

I hold her hand, stroke its veined maps,
places too I've been,

impossible to save her from the detonation
of time bombs after plaques and tangles in her brain.

I put my arms around her and try not to weep, the daughter
who is singing lullabies to put her mother to sleep.

Golden slumbers kiss your eyes ... smiles await you when you rise
Hush little baby don't you cry ...

I try to stay in the moment
hold her like my child

as the hours,

the days

slip by.

Jennifer Matthews

APOCRYPHA

Enthusiasts of stitching, with a *grá* for the meek
imagined a kind of worship
in the singular mismatched blocks
seen in Amish quilts:
an errant colour, or a shape twisted
contrary to the larger pattern
newly christened *humility blocks*
      or mistakes by design,
       a denial of human perfection,
          lucrative, too,
the homely imitations
became keepsake myths, available in any
decent craft store.

      What's the artefact? A heartland fantasy
of humble confession
and our true perfection safely hidden:

the thread and ink of our oldest stories.

Máighréad Medbh

FREETER*

He might be deeply moral, interred
within Rousseau's paradigm, convinced
of the contract's benign guarantee.

For what do we perform any task?
He senses a whirlpool, everything
circling the drain on a pull-through string.

In the digital hive, one is all.
Why should he do what another will?
Euphonic transports are for all ears.

Happenings in the head are concrete.
The neo-shaman says so. He trawls
the states all night and dreams in the day.

He kills nothing, can be still, staring
for hours at a spider, like a poet
whose name he's lost, or was it a film?

A dog's life needs no justifying.
Devotion buys the right to a bed.
He didn't request incarnation.

He often feels like a melted mind,
rivering round hard and fast concepts,
grains of them sticking like silent silt.

Flâneur of his bedroom, year on year.
Stealthily, it seems to his parents,
meaning subverted necessity.

It's unnatural, they conclude, but
let him stay, and coddle him somewhat.
Their genetic investment, treasure.

Dully aching, they steer the subject
to his many gifts, and slice the bread,
their desperate signing for 'future'.

* *Japanese term for someone who eschews the career path in favour of part-time and intermittent employment.*

Geraldine Mills

TAKING ITSELF BACK

Give this house a year
and the wild will reclaim its own.

Already, bats fornicate inside the cladding,
fly through twilight-spin to midge-fest.

Goats' willow, fluent in the language of survival,
notches seed in a gryke of pathway, sprouts.

Leafcutter bees have sawn
leaf-rounds from primrose, verbena,

stuffed them into every crevice of the gable-end
with the same precision a dentist packs a filling,

sealing in their precious future
while snails bivouac underneath the sills.

Someday, a brace of hunters will battle briars,
like heroes in a Grimm's text.

Find walls held up by the tensile strength of web,
swallows in eaves, eggs hatching all over the house,

No trace of the men and women who
held wildness within themselves

and bargained with nature to keep its distance
as long as they lived there.

Nothing but a midden of empties on the back step
where squirrels partied on hazelnuts.

Geraldine Mitchell

GHOST MOTH
Hepialus humuli

Its wings leave smudges on
the windowpane, thin dust rising
as it butts the glass, the moon
behind it and my lamp within.
I have been thinking too much

of my mother, gone these twenty years,
imagine she's come back to visit me.
What is it you want? Aren't you dead
long enough to leave me now,
to take your rest? I turn

the light out, watch the creature
crawl, pause, crawl – looking,
looking where to go next. I lie
and let it watch me too, wait
to see who's first to blink,

think of her old coat
that smelled of comfort, dust and
Sundays – grey fur sleek as moonstone,
downy as the small grey hen
this morning at the market. I perch

restless on a varnished pew,
my cheek afloat on her sleeve,
listen for the sky's deep breath, hear
the hiccupping sea pour bucket-
fuls of water on the shore.

Geraldine Montague

HAY LOFT

Cautiously, we rose
up stones steps,
the slabs almost snug together,
to that other world.
Sunlight filtered
through wooden slits,
motes dancing in its shafts,
hazy light wrapped around
dusty harnesses,
a polished scythe,
the stored bits of that other time.
Stiff bolts yielded
and another door opened
on the thrum of the thresher,
drifting, choking chaff,
tension sizzling along invisible wires
while bags filled
and bales trudged through.

Hours later,
winter sorted,
mugs of hot tea
sealed a perfect day.

Mary Montague

THE TAKING OF CHRIST
after Caravaggio
for Pat Boran

A spasm of moonlight reveals the sway
of resolve as the mob collides and clutches.

Christ's blanched face parries the kiss
while shadowy fists yank at the flare

of a wine-blood cape that threatens to fall
on the heads of both betrayer and betrayed;

thus John is flight at the last. Iscariot
shrugs off the law's reach; but the soldiers –

spurred by intrigue's sign and seal, armoured
by the black and white of direct orders –

are forcing through the confusion, ripping
through love's soft tissue to grasp

at the taut core. Beneath all eyes, the scene's plinth,
its fulcrum: Christ's braced hands.

He quells his wince. Shutters his eyes.
His moon-daubed face founders

with turbid assent. Judas, too late, sees it –
flushes a furtive *Save me!* But Jesus

cannot save. He can only let the treachery sear;
the grief gut. He will yield. The rest must follow

their own ends; like the young man, fallen
behind as the pack surged, leaving him, like us,

the drama's guest, lifting a weak lamp
that merely lights his own face.

Teri Murray

The Last Time I Saw Paris

A summer evening in Paris
the electric beats fills the streets
and even the great cathedrals
of Notre Dame and Saint Denis
hum and sway and sing
and the bells of Saint Germain/Auxerrois
are ready to chime.

For tomorrow there will be a wedding,
a catholic bride to a protestant groom.

But they hide in the shadows, hooded
deaf to the music, hearts hardened against
any sounds of joy.
Their weapons strapped
under jackets
armoured beneath
t-shirts and jeans

as they creep through the streets.
Only the instruments used for prejudice
and terror, unleased, ready for the blood-letting
until the bobblestones of the city
will keen and mourn, the drum struck silent.

II

And dumb.
The drum struck silent
and dumb.

Catherine de Medici, who once the queen,
sipped from a goblet of red wine,

throws an old shawl over the head
and mingles with the crowd.

The Cardinal of Lorraine, of the House of Guise,
drinks his cognac as he paces the floor
and waits for news of deaths of old enemies,
treacherous friends
and any and who stand in the line of fire.

It is the 24th day of August 1572.
It is Saint Bartolomew's Eve.

Emma Must

LAGAN KINGFISHER

That flash of turquoise catching the edge
    of vision of my weak left eye belonged
not on this January towpath but
    in the Amazon, perhaps, or a fable
or the future or – in the form
    of a mosaic of mirrored fragments –
adorning the top of a trinket tin on a stall
    in a bazaar in Jaipur, say, or Marrakesh
and, now I think of it, that stoic heron
    hunching its shoulders in the gentle winter sun
seemed extraordinary too, not to mention
    the adolescent cygnet – that pair of swans! –
flexing their necks in the miracle current.

Joan McBreen

THE STONE JUG

Your last morning in Tullybeg.
You came four thousand miles,
as swallows flying before
you have done.

In cold rain after you left
I walked to Rusheenduff.
Only a handful of flowers would do –
bird's foot-trefoil, self-heal.

I put these wild flowers
of the west in a stone jug
on my window-sill. Without map
or atlas I sent them to you.

Aoibheann McCann

GREY HAIRED AT B & Q

I saw you at B & Q
one Sunday morning
in the outdoor section.
I was wearing my daughter's
hooded sweatshirt.
She is the same age
now, as we were then.

My hair was long
and yours was too,
when we crashed a wedding
at the Warwick,
and stole sandwiches,
too young to be gluten free or vegan.
Then you stole a bike
and I rode on the handlebars
back to Whitestrand.
I went to bed remembering
your face under the quiet streetlight.

Years later
you told me you wanted
to kiss me that night.
I imagined if you had,
the streetlight would have lit our way
for a while
then fizzled out.

At B & Q, grey haired
we exchange small talk
about parts for greenhouses
and drive home in separate
directions in the rain.

Shirley McClure

You Stayed On

I left the party early. Already
it was getting out of hand.
One woman liked to shake
her breasts about – they were
long and unlikably white,
with nipples like rose hips
that butted at the other dancers
in the dangerous light.

Loud laughter woke me,
you'd brought the party back.
Through the wall the talk
was all about the kissing game.
I listened closer, heard how
they'd passed liquor
mouth to mouth, screeching
as they listed names.

I knew you'd taken part,
I even knew whose lips
you'd tasted – that streel
with the tubular breasts,
yes hers, and so I shouted –
I can hear you! And the whole
house fell silent.

Mamo McDonald

GROWING OLD DISGRACEFULLY

There was a time
I wrapped the bath towel tightly round me.
Dressed and undressed
under the tent of my nightie,
and never wore shiny shoes
in case they reflected my knickers.

Now with the nonchalance of age
I sashay from bathroom to bedroom
dressed only in my birthday suit.
Anoint my body with fragrant oils
and treat myself to scarlet lingerie
for my own celebration of Christmas.

I have not done it yet.
But some night soon
I will hop into bed, like Marilyn,
wearing only Chanel No 5,
and my panic button
– just in case.

Vivienne McKechnie

STILL

Clearing out a cupboard, I find you.
Wings closed tight, dusty, dirty looking
moth eaten! The pun lost in the silence.
I lift you out and lie you, flat and still
resting lightly in the palm of my hand.

At first I think of death, winter's trophy,
Caught but forgotten, cold pressed and still.
Then I remember hibernation –
Deep sleep, death's counterfeit. All that –

I move you to the windowsill sun
and some strength sends you upright.
You pause, wait –
wings still closed –
till glimpse of orange petticoat –
tiny trembles of antennae –
shivers sending signals of life
as the sun unshutters your wings
and teased by air, they open and close.
And you are gone!
Flash of orange and black
unfolding in the blue sky.

Later I walk in the spring sun,
step lighter over new green grass.
One or two yellow daffodils open.
Snowdrops bunch around the trees' base.
And, as lambs call, I open my coat
winter closing behind me.

Ellie Rose McKee

SOUNDS

Gently cracking ice
in the pond out back
slowly melting.

Creaking stairs and floorboards
in the old house
as it settles into the ground for the night
and the heat from the dying fire easing out.

The tiny sigh
of a dog in its sleep.

A wonderful host of sounds
that too often go
unnoticed
unheard
unloved.

Maria McManus

A NIGHTINGALE
i.m. Marie Wilson

/.... to think of you –
the delicate cathedral of your body;
your life a flyleaf
in a dense November hymnal of histories;

grim confetti

on a broad church;
an island town,
half-remembering.

Denise Nagle

A PROPOSAL

that each tree type in the neighbourhood wood be QR coded,
to enhance the experience of the visiting public.

Forget the eye, its meandering trail along limbs
of beech, leaves that lap lime green and silvered
across the spring forest, that lift and sift
the powdery essence of bluebell and sorrel,

blend here and there to a sumptuous suffocation –
the gorgeous bombardment of gorse-scent – then
drift away like smoke through the canopy.
Forget the etiquette of light and shade

its geometry through columns of ash where slant sun
plucks the motes of this place. The ear needn't hear
faint crackles on the forest floor or, overhead,
the lore of birds through fitful song.

Each tree is QR coded, the forest is uploaded,
be wary of roots, wear proper boots,
forget, forget, forget.

Joan Newmann

Your Thigh Bone Connected to …

nothing whatsoever.

Do they place them criss-crossed
in a charnel house
'til they dry?

Do they bury them
in a communal grave?

I don't want
my thigh bone
to lie
cheek-to-jowl
with the thigh bone
of someone
I have never met

or with all of the people
I have met.

Bar a few.

Kate Newmann

RAW

For ten years I meant to write an elegy
for Dr Mark Heath, who,
after the first plane slammed,
looked up to see the North Tower
cough out – not just rubble and death
glass metal shrapnel bodies,
parts of bodies, pages and ash –
and who ran towards
the unthinkable to try to help,
his camera rolling, his voice telling
how he was setting up
a trestle table, as close as he could
to the quick of hurt,
an impromptu surgery.

A bakelite-black-crackling reception
and Dr Mark Heath, I believed,
as light gave up to particles of loss,
had given us, on record,
voicelessness,
the choked instant of his own cessation.

In the Metropolitan Museum of Art
Degas' bronze ballerinas held their birdlike poise
and Chagall's floating brides
could not help us comprehend
the living flinging themselves
into the longest gasp of sky
which moved their limbs,
intricate insects drowning in the vertical.

But Dr Mark Heath, I am amazed,
Dr Mark Heath, cardiac anaesthesiologist,

is alive and arguing
that if the death penalty
– which he cannot condone –
if the death penalty involves a lethal jab
– potassium chloride to seize up the heart –
then
a *vast* quantity of anaesthetic *must* be administered
to stop feeling the heart stopping.

Úna Ní Cheallaigh

THE LETTER

Every day without fail, he sends you a letter.
You put them all for safe keeping
in a satin pouch braided with gold chord,
corners looped like lovers' knots;
embroidered in chain stitch – the letter A.

On the morning after the assassination
of the Duchess and Archduke in Sarajevo:
Don't worry my dearest Annie, he writes,
Sweetheart, it will surely come to nothing.

You put on hold the flood of telegrams
being sent from your switchboard
on behalf of the Empire;
fill the chamber of the royal mail's
fountain pen, with black ink.

You ignore the lurch in your stomach,
respond to his foolish words of love.
You crumple the notepaper in your fist,
throw it like a dice on the chequered floor.

And by return of post, you send to him
fondest sweet nothings, in Morse code.

Dairena Ní Chinnéide

THE THIRD EYE

Looking back
there is a road to the bosom of the sky
no barriers, just clouds
that is where my hope lies
imprinted on a blue sky
an eternal horizon
no daily grind
no judgment of fools.

This is the cozy nest of my soul
the core of my story
the peace of truth
where dancing naked is permitted
sanctuary from a world, deaf
to the frequency of my difference.

Out in front
is the sky of the future
the expanse of sea
an uneasy prophesy in my eye
I imagine fierce creatures in those clouds.

But there is a third insight
we are one under the cloak of the universe
through our pain a new tune will come
carried by a gull on the wind
planting a seed in the earth
that will release a spark
from a voice that lives
in the hidden space
seen by the third
eye of the soul.

AN TRÍÚ SÚIL

Ag féachaint siar
tá bóthar go baclainn spéire
gan chonstaic ach scamaill
is ann atá mo dhóchas
greannta ar spéir ghorm
íor síoraí spéire
gan sailiú saoltachta
ná breithiúnas na n-óinseach.

Seo nead theolaí m'anama
áit is ceadmhach rince nocht
de shíor ag fiosrú port nua
tearmann ar shaol atá bodhar
ar mhinicíocht m'éagsúlachta.

Amach chun tosaigh
tá spéir an tsaoil atá le teacht
is fairsinge na mara
tá tuar corraitheach im' shúil
taibhsím ainmhithe allta sna scamaill
nochtaithe ó bhroinn m'aigne.

Tá an tríú léargas ann
mar is ionann sinn uilig fé bhrat na cruinne
mar eadrainn cumfaidh pian port
a iompróidh faoileán ar an ngaoth
a chuirfidh síol sa talamh
a scaoilfidh saor smior splaince
ó ghuth a mhaireann
sa spás sioraí ceilte
a chíonn súil eile
an anama.

Nuala Ní Chonchúir

HARRY KERNOFF REPLIES TO AN ACCUSER

Prolific is not quite
the right
word.

Creative might be
a better
one.

LABHRANN HARRY KERNOFF AMACH

Torthúil?
Níl sé
sin beacht.

Cruthaitheach –
sea,
sin é é.

Colette Ní Ghallchóir

ESCAPE

Can we slip away
from this place
before the lace curtains
of the neighbours fall?
Can we evade
the disapproving eyes
of those rabbits
hopping through the bogholes
on the boundary?
Can we say our goodbyes
to the backstabbing gossips
who are crushing our love
to death?
Or will we bury
this love somewhere
out near the old house
under a scraw of sorrow,
beneath a sod of hate,
in the hope that
the sweet flowers of spring
will grow from it again?
It will lie there peacefully
for ever and a day
until it sprouts
some time
as before:
without knowing,
without warning,
without welcome,
and without fruit.

Translated by Nuala Ní Dhomhnaill

ÉALÚ

An dtig linn an baile seo a fhágáil
go dtí go dtiteann cuirtíní beaga na gcomharsan?
An dtig linn éalú ó shúile
coimhéadach na gcoinín sin
atá ag léimnigh tríd chaorán
seo na teorann?
An dtig linn slán a fhágáil
ag lucht na cúlchainte
atá ag brú bás ar ár ngrá,
nó an gcuirfidh muid
an grá seo
amuigh udaí ag áit an tSeantí,
faoi scraithe an bhróin,
faoi chréafóg seo an fhuatha,
é a chur síos
sa dóigh go bhfásfaidh
blátha bána an earraigh
aníos air,
luífidh sé ansin go suaimhneach
ar feadh na gcianta,
go dtí go bhfásfaidh sé arís,
lá éigin,
mar a d'fhás sé cheana,
gan fhios,
gan choinne,
gan iarraidh,
gan fháilte agus gan bhláth.

Doireann Ní Ghríofa

THE RUSSIAN BROOCH
for Eavan Boland

Astray at the back of your aunt's wardrobe,
under silk sleeves, long skirts, second-hand heels,
a red, vintage coat, lies the Russian brooch

that she bought for a fiver in an antique shop. 'I couldn't
leave it after me', she shrugged. Its glister is long-faded,
its pin bent out of shape, and where once three little stones

must have glowed, now there are only holes. I suppose
they were plucked by a stranger, bartered on the banks
of the Нева́ in Санкт-Петербу́рг, for food or safe passage.

The brooch is deaf now, to all but its memory of the tune
hummed by the first body that held it. It lies, still, at the back
of the wardrobe, recalling the pulse-melody hummed by a

distant heart, a nocturne, perhaps, an air that will never return.

AN BRÓISTE RÚISEACH
for Eavan Boland

Imithe amú ag cúl vardrúis d'aintín, (faoi mhuinchillí
síoda, sciortaí fada, cóta dearg athchaite, bróga athláimhe
ar shála arda) luíonn an bróiste Rúiseach a cheannaigh sí

ar chúig phunt i siopa seandachtaí. 'Ní fhéadfainn é a fhágáil
i mo dhiaidh', dúirt sí. Tá gile a loinnreach maolaithe le fada,
an biorán lúbtha as riocht, is mar a bhíodh seoidíní tráth, níl

anois ach trí pholl loma. Is dócha gur bhain méara strainséara
iad, gur díoladh iad faoina luach ar bhruach oighreata an Нева́
i Санкт-Петербу́рг, ar mhaithe le greim nó gluaiseacht.

Tá an bróiste bodhar anois ar gach ach cuimhne sheanphort
an chéad choirp a chaith é. Luíonn sé fós ag cúl an vardrúis,
ag cuimhneamh siar ar cheol nach bhfillfidh anois go deo

na ndeor, an cuisle-cheol a bhuail brollach strainséara dó fadó.

Colette Nic Aodha

Refrain

Stay away from men
Praise be to God

Avoid alcohol at all costs
Through the mercy of Jesus we will find peace

Whatever else don't take up fags
The Saviour is near to hand

Say 'No' to all types of laziness
Glory be to the King of the Heavens

Give carnal urges and desire the red card
Praise be to Jesus Christ

Avoid lusting after men of your acquaintance
Shine Your light Lord on those of us who still sit in darkness

Let not a scurrilous remark fall from your lips
Send me your Spirit O Lord to guide and comfort me.

AINTEAFAN

Seachain na fir
Moladh le Dia

Seachain an t-ól
Tríd an tiarna is ea a bheidh bua agus glóir

Seachain na toitíní
Tar chugainn dár sábháil

Seachain ainmhian agus drúis
Móraigí an Tiarna ár nDia

Seachain fir ar m'aithne a shantú
Tabhair solas, a Dhia, dóibh siúd atá ina suí sa doircheacht

Seachain na focail fheanntacha a éalaíonn ó mo bhéal
Chuir chugam d'Eagna, a Thiarna,
chun go mbeidh sí ag cuidiú is ag comhoibriú liom.

Edna O'Brien

Watching Obama

2004
You glided on
A swank
With a lava of language,
Prince Hamlet himself in Illinois.
Met your ghosts and raised them –
In belted sackcloth
Chill smiles
A screed of ancient wrongs.
Met the living too '
Who feared your witchcraft
And bought daggers
And several sets of masks.
How far you were meant to travel
Cutting through swathes of sky
Losing or gaining an hour
Puzzling the sad and savage things.
Rivers far below
The taupe earth
Signatures of heaped snow.
You emerged each time
Debonair
As though from a game of tennis.
The sad, the savage things.
The Ones who waited on the roadsides
Believing you would come,
Waited
And were plenished.
They were the ones who brought you hence
As you had brought them
In a beautiful, baffling synthesis.
Now you are Home
Brief is the banquet

A Godsent slumber.
Do you dream of heroic boyish deeds
In some vacant lot, long ago
And do you now begin to fold those dreams
Inside that gaudy Gauguin shirt
And bury them
Under bales of blissful snows.
Your tailor has arrived
To measure you for a breastplate
And a yeoman's greatcoat.
Beyond the tumult
And the fanfare,
Beyond the anointing,
There is the Quiet room
That some call a cell
Where poets weave epiphanies
To the ranunculus
That resembles the rose:
And to the tree of atrocities.
There monks kneel on stone
And pray for nothingness.
There the Chalice
Staring straight at you
Like the sphinx stone-eyed,
Not saying a word,
Not even a nod
And weighs a ton.

Éimear O'Connor

HEANEY'S SYMPOSIUM
National Concert Hall, April 2014

Like monkish figures communing in the Book of Kells
twelve poets onstage;
facing the music.

Incantations spring from every syllable,
ancient and forever grieving,
as if gathered in the pages of the past.

A symposium; it might have been something else,
somewhere else,
had time decided differently?

Among them
but outside them,
a heart lies blown open.

Overhead,
a pencil portrait.
A vague shadow of a vital life.

The end comes.
All that's left is a ghost line,
and his life's work forever forged in paper furrows.

Mary O'Donnell

On Reading My Mother's Sorrow Diary

(The counsellor said 'God wanted him'.
'I wanted him more', she replied and left).

The diary was the thing, labelled
'Sorrow, no laughter in these pages',
double underlined.

I expected smoking syntax, tirades
against her daughters. Instead, she wrote of loss,
the felling of trees; herself split in two

and feeling useless, but happy when we visited,
happier still if we were happy.
She despised the holiday with us, her idea;

'Never again' to a car journey from Malaga
to Jeréz ('filthiest town I've ever seen'),
and she'd scream if my husband attempted

Spanish one more time, his *Gracias Senõr*s
alarm-bells of grating over-eagerness
within the fortress of her well-travelled

knowledge. Mostly, she wrote from day to day.
'A good day. Did some shopping'.
'God when will this end, when will we be together?'

She blessed us, her daughters;
her paper refused harsh words, what there was,
scrupulously overlaid with her code,

an apple, an apple, an apple,
the surefire way to make illegible.
We remained her lovely girls, no slight to us

while even in grief she edited herself.

Liz O'Donoghue

SUNRISE KATHMANDU

The monks' unearthly chant
resonates through the silence
of the drowsy valley
while the sun's first fingers
touch Buddha
and the golden green slopes below.
From the foot of Swayambunath
their gentle sonorous drone
their deep grave mantra
their low reassuring hum
turns tranquil pleasure
to spiritual wonder.

From the bathroom
I return to your bed
and burrow through the sheets
to reach you
until once again wrapped
in our enchanted world.

Una O'Higgins O'Malley

TWENTIETH CENTURY REVISITED

It isn't comfortable to be revisionist
stare into the eyes of a lost leader
while questioning his values,
take down the busts of heroes from their columns
and lose them in the attics of the memory,
remove their pictures from the walkways of the mind,
pass by their monuments. But it may be
that they were premature in their ambitions;
and when the blood was young and hot, with pulses racing
they undertook a war of separation
which might have been avoided.

Maybe this blood-stained century
now should be granted leave of absence
or amnestied in mothballs,
and the indomitable Irishry of North and South
should gaze into the faces of their children
and not their ancestors
while planning for the future.

Geraldine O'Kane

THEN WE WERE FOUR
for Mary

You pop up in daydreams,
night dreams and meditations;
as a child, my guardian angel, a teenager.
Lately you are a twenty-something with glasses,
long almost-black hair, looking like
all three of us, jaw a little longer, squarer.

Sometimes I think you Godlike,
we will never see the face of you – our sister.
Some day we will all be gods.

Nessa O'Mahony

A BEACHCOMBER'S MANUAL
On reading that Irish students are asked
to abandon arts for 'stem' subjects

Nacre is the noun to use
for the irrisdescent inner lining
of bivalves and molluscs.
Nacreous, the adjective.
Don't worry how that sounds:
words weren't built for euphony.
No matter that it whiffs
more of the grave
than of the milky prism
of creams, blues
glistening as the tide recedes
through bladderwrack.
Dreamers gave us mother of pearl
and you know what trouble
dreams got us into.
Stick to the facts,
google if unsure.
But for reason's sake
don't make things up;
metaphors are obsolete
these post-factual days.

Mary O'Malley

SPELL

Tweet tweet tweet. Sometimes the pecking sound
is all there is, sometimes the meme.
In the meaning, sometimes the warning.
Me me me me, me me meme. *Hey little darling
tweet tweet tweet*. The world is fifteen
much crossed, less kissed. *Hey little sweetheart
hate hate hate* sings the man in the machine.

The grown-ups, bewitched for years, immune
in their armchairs in Gleann na mBodhar
to the shrieks of the magical wars
are waving Hamelin's children down the drain.

* *Gleann na Mbodhar is the Valley of the Deaf where Cuchulainn was taken
so that he couldn't hear the war being conjured to lure him to his death.*

Siofra O'Meara

THIS LOOKS BAD

The gettin' ready.
And the goin' out.
And the – I've been told to watch my mouth.
The boys, the drinks, the laughs I've had.
If my mother knew?
Drive her MAD!
Pissin' in the street. Gettin' sick everywhere.
Jesus. I don't fuckin' care.
Gettin' messy on nights out.
Those fights, I can't remember now.
High heels, low cut shirts,
A cheeky naggin never hurts.
The boy at the bar who was alright at the time –
But now?
He's not looking too fine …
Drunk kisses and –
You've a missus?
Spray tans and cheap cans,
Sittin' in a field livin' for the sesh,
All those promises of drinking less.
But promises. Are made to be broken.
And here giz a bit of whatever you're smokin'
My head is dizzy and my eyes are blurred –
And – I DIDN'T KNOW HE HAD A BIRD!
Standin' line for a kip or a club –
And doing a line in a kip of a club,
And rubbin' my arse off some ugly mug,
Being asked do I want a drink –
Replying with a shrug,
Givin' a hug to *that bitch in my year,*
Who I don't really like,
But I'll take a selfie with her –

Always that one woman cryin' in the bathroom screaming
– Why can't I be as pretty as you?
To her poor mate who's holding back her hair,
And I'm doing that drunken stare.
When your face feels numb.
And you're swaying from side to side. And –
EVERYONE IS BEAUTIFUL!
But especially me.
I say staring into my front cam. Whilst having a pee.
And I can't see straight. But I better re-do my eye liner.
And lipstick too!
Has anyone seen my other shoe?
And the dance floor – is wild. With men on either side.
Fightin' for my attention, I choose one, the other gutted
with rejection –
Because on a night out I am usually …
Perfection.
I JUST GOT MY TAX BACK –
Drinks on me!
Snapchat story on a 140 –
Time for a key and –
– She's way too drunk, get her a coffee.
– No, she's just diabetic and her sugars are low.
– Are you tryin' to have a go?
Boys smashin' bottles over each other's heads.
Fuck – I think it's time for bed.
But not before – Maccy D's.
Curly fries, get in me please!
Coughin' up a lung from smokin' like a choo choo train,
Runnin' in the rain down O'Connell street singin'
Dirty old town! Dirty old town!
WAKE UP.
Next day. Voice feelin' hoarse.
Text – At it again tonight?
Reply – Of fucking course!
Because the party never ends!
Not for me!

Leanne O'Sullivan

THE STATION MASS

Everything scrubbed down and scrubbed again.
Every room followed its own lighted passage,
singing out its corners and the polished dark.
The makeshift altar set, she moved from room
to room, pelting the floors with her slippered walk.

Down in the kitchen the beautiful spread of meals,
the little locks and curls of butter flaring sunlight.
We were like her sentry guards in doorways,
bare-foot, sweeping for motes and blemishes
or eyeing hiding places that suddenly stood clear.

Roses, silver, lace. The glasses breathed against.
Then the gravel-call of priest and neighbours
up the lane and we were all come and go again,
herself gone ahead of us down the last swept path,
snapping incantations, scattering light.

Sarah Padden

KEENING

These days of cabins
and fires without a grate of restraint
    of mountain roads split by grass
    of small windows framing sheep
gathered under reaching trees
in stone-walled dells,
are nearly gone.
These last days slip away unremarked
like spring water
    from your untended well
    overrun with reeds and mire.
What was once sacramental, ennobled
    now flushes away quartz-slabs
    mutating the yard into sucking mud
around your endangered home.
These decaying days of undying rain driven into
rotting thatch split chimney
from hearth
    dampening the fire for the first time
    since your father carried the flame
    from his birthplace.
Those days were recasting you for wilderness.
We witnessed your last hours on bog
you were born into
whilst jackdaws murmured above you
ice and fog shrouded Nephin
to ensure you were not taken to modernity
on a cold trolley
then interred on *St Joseph's* to slip away
unnoticed behind a thin curtain.

Nell Regan

LEGACY

My grandmother learned
to write in sand
in which she traced
her name.
       Then,
smoothening grains
with outstretched
palm
she again began.

Mary Ringland

SHORN

Your room replete with heady blooms.
A reckless opulence, the scent
of loved ones' impotence
to stem the tide, rearrange the moon.

You feign surprise at my bouquet
hold it tight, breathe it in,
show me your scar, a scythe's swipe,
from left to right, a savage pruning.

You count your blessings,
relieved to have it out
and longer days, as if earth's axis
swung it just for you, a season
of unfurling light cutting back the night.
You start to fade and walk me to the door.

I leave and wonder will you
daily snip at petals splayed,
pluck out heads curled brown.
Or will you gather up, display
with pride what has survived,
Camellia leaves waxed with resolve,
and the sanguine bark of Dogwood shorn.

Connie Roberts

MOTHER VISITS THE ORPHANAGE

Would you like to come home and live with us again, pet?
No, Ma, I'm grand here.

Your father would be very happy.
You know you're his favourite.
No, Ma, honest, I'm grand here.

He really misses you.
He cries at night by the fire.
I'll write letters to him, Ma.

He'll give up the drink if you come home.
Sure, amn't I grand here, Ma.

Please, child, he'll stop beating me if you come home.
I'm sorry, Ma.

If he kills me, I'll come back and haunt you.

Jane Robinson

LINES FOR A RESCUE
After the life's work of conceptual artist Bas Jan Ader (1942–1975)

All night she's watched and re-watched him climb the indistinct, thin branches of a tree filmed near Amsterdam. As she puts herself in the lacework of his tree she forgets to breathe. Hold tight! Don't jump! Breathe! Don't drown! Is this ache-all-over-the-body some kind of dying? Is this forgetting-to-breathe the false calm of nervous systems shutting down?

In the film, Jan jumps into the canal – his hand lets go that last branch, twigs snap, t-shirt billows and he falls, falling forever in grey-tone, face turned aside.

Libations of ink and milk, and seaweed hand picked off stones where they found Jan's boat, half underwater, with him aged thirty-three lost at sea. *In search of the miraculous* he sailed alone, on a 12-foot boat, from the torch-lit night of LA to the lighthouse of home. Pitfall predicted. Why search for miracles at sea, a project gone wrong, or did Jan know he would drown and enter the dream?

It plays in her head – when he reached for the boat it had drifted, waves washed his face and the stars dimmed like lights seen through rain when the wipers break.

She's kept watch too late, trying to guess why she sketched his jump, scumbled his body, painted his boat underwater. Obsessed. Collaged seas into currents and surges, laid thick ochre ropes like blood hawsers. Physics, gravity, physical perfections hold us together. Do we see the tree-branched nature of life – dreams, decision points, predictions?

From the camera no last shot of his fall from the boat and no picture of his grab for the line but these lines. Many years later, a link – miracle almost perceived.

Moya Roddy

TAKING IN THE WASHING

Fingers numb, I hoist the pole.
Each garment pegged to dry
hangs in a straggled row like
letters in a foreign alphabet.
A wind whips through them,
shyly at first, then with gusto –
a swirling gypsy dance of colour,
arms and legs flying.

Darkness falls. I rush outside,
find an early frost has set to work.
Stiff and shrivelled now – like dried
fruit or the cast-off skins of aliens –
I can't bring them in to melt and
drip on my carpet. Let them stay out
all night, the sun can thaw them
in the morning.

Rounding the gable I stop.
Between two firs a full moon
dangles. Hurrying back,
I haul them down, bend
their freezing forms
to my warm body.

Rosemarie Rowley

THE HARDEST TIME

It is the hardest time of all to be living
The worst of both systems, and now the threat
Of daily interface with terror, giving
Innocent people a shocking untimely death

Doctrine from the right and from the left
But the same people in power it seems
What happened to the warp and weft
Of our adolescent and childish dreams

Now a gun talks more than a friend
The lonely hours are spent in solitude
Trust has come to a bitter end
As we fail to register our gratitude

And fear stalks us all, we could be next
Depending on a call or a text.

Mary Ryan

The Club

We are a club now of your discarded women.
Like cigarettes you have dragged us into you,
made us your project
nurtured and fondled us.

You have hopped from one to the other
the latest being made to feel
she has landed the prize salmon.

When you are jaded
you have not the kindness to stump us out.
Instead you leave us smouldering on an ash-tray.

We suffer for your inadequacies.

Deirdre Shanahan

SCARVES

When I arrive, you always have your hat and coat on
ready to go
like a little girl waiting for the journey.
But you always wore the right outfit;
a pink dress and stilettos for dances,
beaver fur in winter,
a flowery swimsuit for the waves,
trousers as you got older
and, these days, lavish silk scarves
swirling around your neck.

You are still organized,
making your bed and keeping your room sweet
so when I peep in, it is tidy,
clothes are folded across a chair
and medicines on the chest of drawers
laid out in hands reach from the bed.
Every day is like this,
a template of the one ahead,
yet each growing more unrecognizable.
I lived in this house for years
but have not been here before.

It is windy as we leave for the hospital
and daffodils at the far end of the garden
in the breeze
wave goodbye like courtiers
or old boyfriends you used to spend afternoons
telling me about,
while you were ironing our clothes.

Lorna Shaughnessy

THE WIDOW'S SLEEP

When Molly Brady married Hugh Reilly it was a made match. To his hundred acres, stone farmhouse, silver-tipped cane and pony and trap with gleaming tackle, she brought gold sovereigns, a heifer and a trunk of linen. It was 'nothing but the best for his Molly' in Ryan's drapery store in the town.

He died of a heart condition, leaving a widow with seven children, memories and spiralling debts. The thirties bit hard. One morning the children rose to find no fire lit in the range and the chickens still locked up. Their mother was in bed, submerged in so deep a sleep she did not stir when they called and gently tugged at her nightdress. Frightened, they fetched the doctor, who told them on no account to try to rouse her, for fear the shock of waking would do her harm.

When she had slept for two nights and a day, the eldest of the girls sent for a priest from another parish, a childhood friend of their uncle. He told the children to pray, then sat at her bedside, spoke her maiden name, and called deep into her past.

You were the first thing I saw, the days
I cycled to your house up the Church Brae.

You, Molly Brady, always swinging on the same gate
saying your brother was waiting and what had kept me so late?

Some days you came to fish with us, just to look,
though you wouldn't be seen dead threading a worm on a hook.

Your brothers all complained you were your father's pet,
that he even let you eat the best bit off his plate.

They said you cheated when you were on guard
playing forty-forty or kick the tin in the yard.

Later, they grumbled that it wasn't fair
that a girl's chores were much easier than theirs'

but on Sundays not one of them gave out
when neighbours arrived with fiddles and bottles of stout

and you took your concertina from its box.

Do you mind that, Molly?
Can you still play 'Green grows the Holly?'

Will I hum if for you now?
Let me see, how does it go?

Father McGovern did his best to hum the old tune. He saw
no change in Molly's sleeping face. What he could not see,
however, was how the notes entered her ear and sank
deeper and deeper in a healing amnesia that muffled the
voices of her dead husband and her children, silencing the
treacherous world that lay above the submerged land of
sleep.

Molly, Molly Brady do you remember me,
the song you teased from the concertina on your knee?

When you were neither mother, wife nor bride
and not a care in the world entered your young mind,

inside the love and safety of your parents' home.
What sport is there in playing all alone?

A song's only worth the company it keeps
Will you come back to us, will you rouse from this deep sleep?

The song was bait on the fisherman's line that Fr McGovern cast back in time. He trusted the knowledge he had gained in long days of country pursuits and blindly, kept casting and casting, till the song hooked.

She stirred. The priest's breath quickened. He knew not to reel in the line too fast. What was needed here was a slow remembering.

Molly, Molly Brady, will you follow the song
from your parents' kitchen to your own farm,

through heartache and hardship, debt and betrayal
your children are waiting here, fearful and praying.

Molly Reilly emerged slowly and with some confusion, asking where her husband was. The children looked at one another. He was in the byre, they said, and would not be long.

Jo Slade

HIVE

She wished for sweetness
a common cure for heart's hurt.
Where there was sadness
now there'd be no more.

So he bought her honey
in pots the shape of breasts –
as round a curve
would hold life's liquid, gold.

He put them on a shelf –
they glittered, glistened
the pots reflected a convex image
where edges blurred and pain dissolved.

A kind of axis turned the honeyed eye
she saw him, inside the hive –
his wings winnowing
the perfumed air.

Sarah Strong

WIKIPEDIA
in memory of Eithne Strong

Not for myself but for you,
I pass meticulous hours,
vested to preserve your work,
to ensure your place in annals.
A weary bind with scant return,
I ask myself, what is it for?
Will you love me all the more?
Will you enfold me in your arms?

Yet, mothers and daughters struggle
to meet in ways that nurture.
Loving elision is more common,
but oh, to meet as two women.

Mothering myself is what matters most,
this exercise of mine is but a ghost.

Lila Stuart

THE RAISING

She handled each of her thirteen
much the same way she baked her bread:
measuring, folding, smoothing,
scolding, stroking, kneading.

Some bannocks needed the heel of her hand,
others were dimpled with the tips of her fingers.
Wheaten bread – coarse and ridgey
on the outside – soft and squidgy inside.

Treacle bread – exotic, with notions of upperosity.
Soda bread – plain and dependable.
Currant bread – soda bread with
currents of attitude.

The stroke was a left-sided one:
instead of two thumbs smoothing grooves
on the arms of her chair, working out worries,
only her right one rotated now.

When Mass was said at home,
by one of her sons,
her good hand thumped her chest:
Mea cupla. Mea cupla. Mea maxima culpa.

At the raising of the bread and wine,
she lifted her own dead, wrinkled hand
with the other one –
by way of offering.

Lisa C. Taylor

FERRY CROSSING AT INISHMORE

Nothing remains rooted for long
shaft of sun, percussive rain,
a thrum of loss, the moving
in the widening where tide joins sand.

A shaft of sun, percussive rain,
then brindled clouds, a strand of clear
above the widening where tide joins sand,
a cast of dusk unfurls its cape.

Brindled clouds, a strand of clear,
striations of bindweed rim the path.
Cast of dusk unfurls its cape;
ferry muffled in its mooring.

Striations of bindweed rim the path,
a dialect of growing things.
Ferry muffled in its mooring,
blue notes and a noble refrain.

A dialect of growing things
Ferry crossing, the harbour's tongue,
clear notes and a noble refrain,
graphite glide of bank and salt.

Ferry crossing, the harbour's tongue
a thrum of loss, the moving sea,
graphite glide of bank and salt.
Nothing remains rooted for long.

Gráinne Tobin

BORDERING

The native Irish birch is enough to fill a window,
winter branches pluming out of its five-pronged trunk,
holding up our washing line, nestbox, birdbath,
ringing the years before and after ceasefires.

This side of the glass, a Chinese pound-shop cat
is patting the air each second with its golden paw,
ready to knock fists for luck when we come in,
long-lashed human eyes painted wide open –

staring at rolling news as flags change twice in two days,
observing shot and shell and stumbling people –
the clenched paw waves at a reporter pointing
to a map of frontiers with a star marked Scutari,
salutes the antiques expert who's displaying
the lamp Miss Nightingale held to see the wounded,
her Turkish workman's lantern, a flame-lit cylinder
of waxed and pleated linen bought in the souk
at Constantinople, like those still sold in Istanbul.

Jessica Traynor

CHERRY FALL

Spring lights candles
for the city's dead
and in Mountjoy Square

each cherry tree
is a beacon for ghosts.
Here, the corner

where you spoke
of your mother's death,
here the yellow bench

where late and drunk,
enraptured by petals,
you told me

I was becoming
myself again
after so long astray –

where I discovered too late
that you didn't
know me at all.

Here, the tree
we walked beneath
when I decided

I could be whoever
you wanted that night;
that cherry blossom

falls and scatters quickly,
that ghosts can't call us
to account.

Jean Tuomey

WHAT WE COULD NOT SAY

It was not moonlight on the waves
that kept us in conversation,
its reflection walking with us.

It was the moon itself, huge and bright,
a yellow plate on a black cloth.
We talked of when it was last so perfect,

how we longed to be by the sea on nights like this,
of the recent eclipse some of us had slept through,
the years until there would be another.

What none of us could say
was how when the moon was full
he would call us from our homework,

down the gravel path to see the light
through the branches of the sycamore tree.

Mary Turley-McGrath

NALA

was the new wife in the village;
she would help the rains return
and crops grow; they made

love each night in their new hut
and in weeks she was with child;

when the planting season came
she sowed seeds with the others;

prayed as she dropped grains
of maize and millet into solid soil;

she could feel the child stir
in her womb, each day stronger
in the heating landscape;

the seeds took root, she prayed
as they began their fragile life
like tiny colourless ants;

he smiled at her growing belly;
in bed each night she felt his root
grow sturdy until one morning

the stalks had withered;
like last year, he said, kicking the clay;

the ground grew harder; one night
the baby kicked his father's back;
next morning he left.

Bridget Wallace

AT DROIM AN DHROID

*in memory of my uncle, Bill Thompson, and his wife Marjorie,
late of Lettermacaward, County Donegal, June 1998*

Maghery's crimson breastplate
signals the setting of the sun
over Trigena bay,
and in this liminal place
I nestle in the red passion of the rowan trees
as evening's magic shadow show begins.

I hear a wave break
and rumble in the bowels
of the river Finn,
on it rolls to break like my reverie
on the rocks, among the turf brown rills
that flow through Droim la Dhroid.

Above the bridge, the road,
like Jacob's ladder,
rises toward Dungloe
but no angel descends.
Only the bogs beckon,
pillars of turf by day,
at night slashed
by slivers of moon on water.

In the arch of the bridge a spider weaves
a dream-catcher, I will set it with a cockle shell
and seagull feathers, a bowline knot,
and other stranded treasure.
In its fragile net, my nightmares
will perish with the rising tide.
In dreams such things make sense
to children and to lovers.

As night draws in, a solitary mink,
the scourge of salmon fishers,
slips his black tongue
between Finn's lips.
I number him among my metaphors,
he and I are lodged
in these summer verses;
he is king of riverbanks,
I am queen of bridges.

Catherine Webb

Icarus

And so
the story fanned out into history and became legend.
After all the struggle to collect lathes light enough,
shaving thin strips of wood,
robbing nests for discarded feathers,
tying them together with bits of shoelaces,
despairing when they fell apart.

Then finding the dead animal
boiling the hooves to make glue,
rendering the bones and offal for tallow,
working together at this stage,
one holding, the other spreading,
waiting in hope and expectation.

Binding the structure to the boy's arms,
'Take care now and remember
the world will hear', he said
and ran with the boy towards the cliff edge.
'Jump!' he roared and the boy soared
up and up
higher and higher into history,
then the heat and the melt
and the falling.

Mary Barber

To Mrs Frances-Arabella Kelly

Today, as at my Glass I stood,
To set my Head-cloaths, and my Hood;
I saw my grizzled Locks with Dread,
And call'd to mind the Gorgon's Head.

Thought I, whate'er the Poets say,
Medusa's Hair was only gray:
Tho' Ovid, who the Story told,
Was too well-bred to call her old;
But, what amounted to the same,
He made her an immortal Dame.

Yet now, whene'er a Matron sage
Hath felt the rugged Hand of Age,
You hear our witty Coxcombs cry,
Rot that old Witch – she'll never die.
Tho', had they but a little Reading,
Ovid would teach them better Breeding.

I fancy now, I hear you say,
Grant Heav'n, my Locks may ne'er be gray!
Why am I told this frightful Story?
To Beauty a Memento mori.

And, as along the Room you pass,
Casting your Eye upon the Glass,
Surely, say you, this lovely Face
Will never suffer such Disgrace:
The Bloom, that on my Cheek appears,
Will never be impair'd by Years.
Her Envy, now, I plainly see,
Makes her inscribe those Lines to me.
These Beldams, who were born before me,

Are griev'd to see the Men adore me:
Their snaky Locks freeze up the Blood;
My Tresses fire the purple Flood.

Unnumber'd Slaves around me wait,
And from my Eyes expect their Fate.
I own, of Conquest I am vain,
Tho' I despise the Slaves I gain.
Heav'n gave me Charms, and destin'd me
For universal Tyranny.

The Recantation: To the same Lady.

Forgive me, fair One, nor resent
The Lines to you I lately sent.
They seem, as if your Form you priz'd,
And ev'ry other Gift despis'd:
When a discerning Eye may find,
Your greatest Beauty's in your Mind.

forthcoming in Emily O'Flaherty (editor), *Stepping Out of Her Province: The Collected Poems of Mary Barber, Laetitia Pilkington and Constantia Grierson, c. 1885–1755* (Arlen House, 2017).

Laetitia Pilkington

THE PETITION OF THE BIRDS (TO MR PILKINGTON ON HIS RETURN FROM SHOOTING)

Ah Shepherd, gentle Shepherd! Spare
Us plum'd Inhabitants of Air,
That hop, and inoffensive rove
From Tree to Tree, from Grove to Grove;
What Phrenzy has possest your Minds
To be destructive of your Kind?
Admire not if we Kindred claim,
Our sep'rate Natures are the same;
To each of us thou ow'st a Part,
To grace thy Person, Head, or Heart;
The chaste, the fond, the tender Dove
Inspires thy Breast with purest Love;
The tow'ring Eagle claims a Part
In thy courageous, gen'rous Heart;
On thee the Finch bestow'd a Voice,
To bid the raptur'd Soul rejoice;
The Hawk has giv'n thee Eyes so bright,
They kindle Love and soft Delight;
Thy snowy Hue and graceful Mien,
May in the stately Swan be seen;
The Robin's Plumes afford the red,
Which thy soft Lips and Cheeks bespread;
Thy filial Piety and Truth,
The Stork bestow'd to crown thy Youth.
Did we these sev'ral Gifts bestow
To give Perfection to a Foe?
Did we so many Virtues give,
To thee, too fierce to let us live?
Suspend your Rage, and every Grove

Shall echo Songs of grateful Love.
Let Pity sooth and sway your Mind,
And be the Phoenix of Mankind.

forthcoming in Emily O'Flaherty (editor), *Stepping Out of Her Province: The Collected Poems of Mary Barber, Laetitia Pilkington and Constantia Grierson, c. 1885–1755* (Arlen House, 2017).

Constantia Grierson

ON THE ART OF PRINTING
(Lines addressed to the Hon Mrs Percival)

Hail mystic art, which men like angels taught
To speak to eyes, and paint embody'd thought!
The deaf and dumb, blest skill, reliv'd by thee,
We make one sense perform the task of three.
We see, we hear, we touch, the head and heart,
And take or give what each but yields in part;
With the hard laws of distance we dispense,
And without sound, apart, commune in sense;
View, though confin'd, nay, rule this earthly ball,
And travel o'er the wide-extended ALL.
Dead letters thus with living notions fraught,
Prove to the soul the telescope of thought.
To mortal life immortal honour gives;
And bid all deeds and titles last and live
In scanty life – Eternity we taste,
View the first ages, and inform the last.
Arts, history, laws, we purchase with a look,
And keep, like fate, all nature in a book.

forthcoming in Emily O'Flaherty (editor), *Stepping Out of Her Province: The Collected Poems of Mary Barber, Laetitia Pilkington and Constantia Grierson, c. 1885–1755* (Arlen House, 2017).

Eva Gore-Booth

To E.G.R.

All lights are quenched, all joys in darkness drown,
The fog lies heavy on the breathless town,
Ah, come with me and breathe the sunny air
In Jacob Boehme's Garden of roses fair.

Behind the smoke bright towers soar up sublime,
Entombed the unborn flowers wait their time,
Gabriel doth hold a Lily, not a sword,
Are we not guests at the mysterious board?

The River of Life is running strong and free,
White is the May, and all the hyaline sea
Shines suddenly with Christ's mysterious smile ...
Sit by this window, let us watch awhile ...

forthcoming in Sonja Tiernan (editor), *The Collected Poems of Eva Gore-Booth* (Arlen House, 2017).